SELECTED

To my mother, with love and gratitude,
and to the memory of my father

CAROLE SATYAMURTI

Selected Poems

Oxford   New York

OXFORD UNIVERSITY PRESS

1998

Oxford University Press, Great Clarendon Street, Oxford OX2 6DP

Oxford New York

Athens Auckland Bangkok Bogotá Buenos Aires Calcutta
Cape Town Chennai Dar es Salaam Delhi Florence Hong Kong Istanbul
Karachi Kuala Lumpur Madrid Melbourne Mexico City Mumbai
Nairobi Paris São Paulo Singapore Taipei Tokyo Toronto Warsaw
and associated companies in Berlin Ibadan

Oxford is a registered trade mark of Oxford University Press

British Library Cataloguing in Publication Data

Data available

Library of Congress Cataloging in Publication Data
Satyamurti, Carole.
[Poems. Selections]
Selected poems / Carole Satyamurti.
(Oxford Poets)
I. Title. II. Series.
PR6069.A776A6 1998 821'.914–dc21 98–14021
ISBN 0–19–288101–9

1 3 5 7 9 10 8 6 4 2

Typeset by George Hammond Design
Printed in Great Britain by Athenæum Press Ltd.,
Gateshead, Tyne and Wear

CONTENTS

from STRIKING DISTANCE (1994)

BROKEN MOON

BETWEEN THE LINES

I

Words were dust-sheets, blinds.
People dying randomly, for 'want of breath',
shadowed my bed-times.
Babies happened;
adults buried questions under bushes.

Nouns would have been too robust
for body-parts; they were
curt, homeless prepositions—'inside',
'down there', 'behind', 'below'. No word
for what went on in darkness, overheard.

Underground, straining for language
that would let me out, I pressed to the radio,
read forbidden books. And once
visited Mr Cole. His seventeen
budgerigars praised God continually.

He loved all words, he said, though he used
few to force a kiss. All that summer
I longed to ask my mother, starved myself,
prayed, imagined skirts were getting tight,
hoped jumping down ten stairs would put it right.

My parents fought in other rooms,
their tight-lipped murmuring muffled
by flock wallpaper.
What was wrong, what they had to say
couldn't be shared with me.

He crossed the threshold in a wordless
slam of doors. 'Gone to live near work'
my mother said, before she tracked down
my diary, broke the lock, made me cut out
pages that guessed what silence was about.

2

Summer, light at five. I wake, cold,
steal up the attic stairs,
ease myself into Mrs Dowden's bed,
her mumble settling to snores again.

In a tumbler, teeth enlarged by water;
her profile worrying, a shrunken mask.
Her body's warm, though,
smells of soap and raisins.

I burrow in her arm's deep flesh
forgetting, comforted. Finding out
with fingers that creep like stains
that nipples can be hard as pencil ends,

breasts spongy, vaster than a hand's span;
and further down under the nightdress,
a coarseness, an absence;
not what I'd imagined.

3

Chum Larner, Old Contemptible,
badge on his lapel, barbered our hedges
for parade; nipped capers off nasturtiums,
their peppery juice evoking India,
the dysentery that wiped out his platoon,
'But yer can't kill orf a Cockney sparrer!'
His epic stories rattled gunshot,
showed me what dying meant.

The shed—tropical dusk, air thickened
by tarred twine, drying rosemary,
his onion sandwiches. Sitting on his knee
I'd shiver as he told about the ghost
of Major Armstrong's fancy woman
who wandered the cantonment, crooning.
My mother stopped me going,
suspecting him, perhaps, of more than stories.

4

Upstairs was church,
a clock ticking somewhere
and my mother, a penitent,
breasting the stairs,
smile upside-down,
streak of tears
gone when I looked again.

No sound behind the door
I dawdled past on tip-toe,
where strangers were allowed
and where, wanting more than breath,
my grandmother was being dulled
by blue walls, too much sleep,
the brownish, disinfected smell;
by being too delicate to touch,
by no one singing to her,
by hunger, chafing her to bone.

5

'. . . someone for you to play with.'
But I could tell she'd be
useless at throwing, or bricks,
no good at pretending.

'Isn't she sweet?' Couldn't they see
she was yellow, creased, spotty,
an unfinished frog, a leaky
croaky cry-for-nothing?

'Be gentle now!' But I was
doing what they said, playing.
My best doll's bonnet
fitted her floppy beetroot head.

She smelled of powdered egg.
They warmed her vests.
She slept against my mother's skin.
'How do you like her?' Send her back.

6

Books let me move close to them,
breathe their scent of secret places.
They broke through net curtains,
stained glass, tea-time
and dared to shout, take risks
for love or principle.
One was an unsuitable companion,
revealed with disappointing diagrams
the body's *terra incognita*.

People were difficult to read,
foreign, with uncut pages.
I could see their spines braced
to support the weight of hidden words.
Their covers carried all the information
they thought necessary.

In my dream, I always woke
just as I reached to touch
the most beautiful, the only book
that would have shown me everything.

Did I know what I'd find?
I see myself
sneaking, because I must,
across her rose carpet;
turned cat, criminal
without the nerve.

I'm sliding open
the middle drawer
—the letters, wrong
in this habitat of hair-grips,
powder leaves,
the smell of evening gloves.

I can still see
his love-shaped writing,
ink confidently black,
vowels generous
as mouths, fluent
underlined endearments.

And my father's
pinched hieroglyphics,
clipped sentences
the shape of pain
trying to be dignified.
Words pulled out by the root.

Has hindsight twisted it?
I remember no surprise,
only the lurch of knowing
here was the edge
of something absurd,
a terminal complexity.

MOUTHFULS

They lasted longer then.
Mars Bar paper crackled
as we rewrapped half for later,
sliced the rest
to thin cross-sections,
arranged them like wedding-cake
—loaves and fishes.

Sherbet lemons, hard against the palate,
vicious yellow. Strong sucking
made them spurt, fizz, foam,
sugar splinters lacerate
the inside of my cheeks,
surprising as ice crystals in the wind
that cut my legs through socks.

Licorice comfits shaken in a tin
made marching music.
Or they were fairy food
—each colour wrought a different magic:
 mauve for shrinking,
green, the power to fly,
red, the brightest, eternal sleep.

The oddity of gob-stoppers:
tonguing each detail
of the surface—porcelain,
tiny roughnesses,
licking, rolling it, recapturing
the grain and silk of nipple;
rainbows glimpsed only in mirrors.

A shorter life for jelly-babies
—drafted into armies, black ones last,
or wrapped in paper shawls in matchbox beds,
taken out, chewed from the feet up,
decapitated out of kindness
or, squeamishly sucked,
reduced to embryos.

MY FIRST CUP OF COFFEE

I'm sophisticated in my Cuban heels,
my mother's blue felt hat
with the smart feather like a fishing fly

as I sit with her in the Kardomah; and
coffee please, I say, not orange squash,
crossing my legs, elegant as an advert.

Beyond the ridges of my mother's perm
the High Street is a silent film
bustling with extras: hands grasping purses,

steering prams, eyes fixed on lists,
bolster hips in safe-choice-coloured skirts
—and then, centre screen, Nicolette Hawkins

(best in the class at hockey, worst at French)
and a boy—kissing,
blouse straining, hands

where they shouldn't be:
the grown-up thing. My hat's hot, silly;
coffee tastes like rust.

My mother, following my gaze, frowns: common.
I'm thinking, if I could do all that
I could be bad at French.

ERDYWURBLE

My father's parents sold fish.
At school, Greek scholars taunted him,
the scholarship boy,
called him 'bromos', said he stank of fish.
His gifts withered; he learned
a stammer that stayed with him for life,
words jumping like the tiddlers he tried to catch
in the canal.

But from the fractured syllables, there grew
words of his own: 'Don't arrap',
he'd say when we were plaguing him.
'Pass me the erdywurble'—we in giggles
guessing what it was. 'I'm mogadored'
when the last crossword clue eluded him.
'It won't ackle', trying to splint
a broken geranium.

Unable to persuade the doctor
to help him die while he still knew himself,
his words trickled, stopped. Keening continually,
he stumbled on, mistaking night for day,
my mother for his own,
then recognizing no one. Just once,
answering his new granddaughter's cry, he said
'poor kippet'.

PROGNOSES

'She'll walk something like this . . .'
Springing from his chair
he waddles, knees crumpled,
on the outer edges of his feet
—a hunchback, jester, ape,
a wind-up toy
assembled by a saboteur.
I turn away, concentrate
on the caesarean sting.

I wander corridors.

Far off, approaching,
a couple, hand in hand,
the girl, lurching
against the window's light.
I hear them laugh, pick up
the drift—a private joke,
the film they saw last night.
Long after they are gone, I hear
the jaunty click-creak of her calipers.

INTENSIVE CARE

Your voice silenced by tubes,
the mute, continual cough lifts you awake.
I stroke your hair; you stare at me,
eyes remote, tearless.

You write, 'I'm hungry'.
I watch each breath
sucked in between your ribs,
beg for you.

You lie as if in state,
too dignified.
If I thought you were leaving me
from this white room

with only plastic pillows for your journey
I would cram your hands with anemones,
snatch out the cannula, enfold you,
run with you to where the band is playing.

But now, as my hands
make shadow creatures on the wall,
I read your lips: 'rhinoceros',
know I have you still.

GETTING THERE

Sports Day. Miss Cook
had whispered to the rest
to let you win the walking race
and not to tell.

Your jerky gait,
your straining;
the others shuffling behind,
their over-hearty cheers,

you pleased, unsure.
When your friend confessed,
wanting you to be
like anyone again,

you looked bereft,
confused
as if the walls
had changed alignment.

You understand proportion.
I still wake at night
explaining to Miss Cook
why she was wrong

—I know the artfulness
of happy endings:
once when you were small,
still chair-bound,

I dreamed you walked
perfectly into my room;
somehow, even in the dream,
a counterfeit—but so real

I woke shaking, as though
I'd almost been drawn
into a lotus-land
where I'd never find you.

Sometimes, when we're gay,
we hold hands, polka round
like dancing bears,
laughing at each other.

BROKEN MOON

for Emma

Twelve, small as six,
strength, movement, hearing
all given in half measure,
my daughter,
child of genetic carelessness,
walks uphill, always.

I watch her morning face;
precocious patience as she hooks each sock,
creeps it up her foot,
aims her jersey like a quoit.
My fingers twitch;
her private frown deters.

Her jokes can sting:
'My life is like dressed crab
—lot of effort, rather little meat.'
Yet she delights in seedlings taking root,
finding a fossil,
a surprise dessert.

Chopin will not yield to her stiff touch;
I hear her cursing.
She paces Bach exactly,
firm rounding of perfect cadences.
Somewhere inside
she is dancing a courante.

In dreams she skims the sand,
curls toes into the ooze of pools,
leaps on to stanchions.
Awake, her cousins take her hands;
they lean into the waves,
stick-child between curved sturdiness.

She turns away from stares,
laughs at the boy who asks
if she will find a midget husband.
Ten years ago, cradling her,
I showed her the slice of silver in the sky.
'Moon broken', she said.

MOTHER'S GIRL

(i.m. *Pat Bain*)

She remembers a mother waving from a train;
'Don't cry, silly girl,
Mother will come back very soon.'

As her life leaches out into still air
she watches tramps shuffle from the park,
knows envy's vertigo.

She hears herself speak clichés: '. . . a nightmare',
sees friends look reassured that dying
can be compared to anything familiar.

'The children will remember me ugly.'
But she is bone-beautiful, a Giacometti,
filigree of veins in yellowed ivory.

She wears parrot colours;
she buys great bags of tulip bulbs,
learns a new Berlioz song, talks of a holiday.

While her husband whispers to the children
she turns the fragile vaulting of her back;
marzipan smile crumbles, tastes of quinine.

A stranger's fingers clutch the furniture
—splinters, fat enough last month to draw
bravura from the piano, coax a baby into sleep.

Dressed for the ward-round she is actress
and audience, hair in a bright bandanna,
watching through ice, marionettes, miming.

Roused by a small hand from morphine dreaming
she murmurs, as she sails the summer night,
'Mother will be better, very soon.'

FROM ROSA IN SÃO MARTINHO

for Maria Pinto

1 *Postcard*

Looping the coast
—mountains, glint of levadas,
banana groves. So many houses!
Touch-down,
finding my face wet.

Shrieks, embraces, presents,
peeping neighbours,
maracujà, honey cake
—and noise! Night:
a lizard winking.

It has to be like this—
feeling my way
through grittiness of soap,
enamel plates, back
into the textures of home.

2 *Blessing*

Not the place I fled from—
this is a peeled, harmless replica.
I'm back, but almost as a tourist;
I don't need, after all,
the city clothes, new black suitcase
to ward off the past.

It's not that I've forgotten my father:
the burn of leather belt on skin,
fear drying the mouth like quince.
It's not that the colours—wine flush
of his eyes, neck's purple veins—
have blurred at all.

I remember how I spat him out, turned
a scarred back against him. Now, I know
I simplified him, censored the vision
of his head—pale strip of forehead
bared to the landlord, hat awkward
in his dirt-stiff hands.

But the memories are flat,
scissored frames from a lost film.
I left in silence, refused
to ask his blessing. Today, easily,
bending to kiss this tearful stranger,
I whisper 'Pai, sua benção.'

3 *Embroidery*

All day I sit cross-legged with the women
embroidering, talking of husbands
—past, present and to be arranged.
Sisters, cousin, aunts, we make the flowers
our mothers showed us, white on white.

Curved spines, rough ankles,
flattened finger-ends—their bodies
moulded to the task, they pull their threads
taut, shape disappointments
into an appliqué of laughter.

At night I hold a phantom needle,
feel my arm still lifting thread, falling.
My eye sees templates everywhere
—the sea marked out with lights of tiny boats,
the sky pricked by stars.

4 *Patching*

No real men here—
only the hopeless stay,
those softened young
by wine for wages—empty men
grown thin as clothes pegs.

Around six yesterday, my sister
laid down her needlework,
took it up, her stitches crazy,
shouted at the children,
stood waiting by the road

for Alfredo, late, staggering
arrogant as a toddler, bawling
a vicious song, wanting her
to punish. She, twice his weight,
allowed him to be strong.

Today, he stayed at home. She hid
her bruises, unpicked stitches,
fed him baby-soup. Tonight, he sits
silent, smoking harsh tobacco,
turning five escudos in his hand.

5 *Futures*

My niece walks with me in moonlight:
'I'll marry an Italian, like my aunt.
He'll be tall, blonde perhaps.
We'll ride a gondola. I'll have
a silver kitchen that works by itself.'
I squeeze her hand. I know
her mother has an eye on Paolo,
neighbour's boy—short, quiet,
working in an office in Machico.
And Fernanda's a sensible girl.

Keen for my reaction, my nephew tells me
he likes calculus. He's quick,
drums his fingers, restless for something.
I imagine him a scientist—know
he'll leave school when he can,
work for an uncle who makes coffins.
Already, in the way he turns his head,
his hooded look, angering his sisters,
there's the old pride that draws on nothing
but itself, and ends by drowning.

6 *Fish*

Shouting, they heave the dead weights
up the ramp, scales flashing,
slap them down on stones, heaped high,
spilling the smell of sea.

Women promenade, size up the catch,
begin the ancient ritual
—clamour for prices, feigned disbelief,
shrewd scrutiny of measures.

The fishermen throw down their caps,
wield hatchets, cleave great tuna
into chunks, rub salt on,
spread them in sun to dry.

My sister shows me off
—her English relative. Neighbours
dissect me with their eyes, whisper
rumours of my past.

Pride of the catch, the black espada,
ugly scabbard fish, leers
as if embarrassed at being caught
dead on a trestle table.

I stare at it: poor oddity.
In my mind's eye, its muscles
leap again; it strikes out, plunges
back to its gypsying.

7 *Photograph*

So that's who she was—
not my collage of gilded fragments,
sugar saint, eyes sea deep,
comforting me, her favourite,
but a plain girl, starved of choices,
whose bones lie hidden somewhere here
anonymous as flints.

In the creased studio photograph
there's pride, a sort of avidness
transfiguring the desperate impatience
my brother says she showed with all of us.
She poses, a star,
embracing her moment
before the shutter snapped.

I have to leave her here,
mother who never was,
be mother to myself.
But I remember reaching up
to hand her clothes-pegs,
laughing with her as we named them
—Manuel, Josè, Vicente, Father João.

8 *Orphanage*

This is where we sat
chasing lice
through one another's hair
sucking marrow bones.
Sometimes, after dark,
I'd slip out
to these plum trees,
shrunken now,
gorge stolen fruit.

I thought I'd find the faces,
frowzy veils
that stifled me for years.
But the house is empty,
stripped of the vast
camphor-smelling armoires,
credences, the cornered saints
whose monstrous shadows
subdued our urge to sing.

I hated them for their pinched
insistence on the rules.
Maybe they believed
there was no better language
they could teach a girl
than that of service,
curbing our tongues, hands, eyes
—His will be done. Today
I would have told them otherwise.

9 Procession

Christ, in his private ecstasy of pain,
parades the streets. The sign-writer
who retouches the gilt from time to time,
the woman who dusts Him every day
stand breathless as He passes.

Earlier they and many others knelt
as I did once, arranging lilies, agapanthus,
marigolds into a patterned carpet
which now the tubby priest,
the bearers of the statue, trample on.

We have lost touch, He and I.
I can't recapture that straightforward love,
though whether it was time, space
or experience that distanced us, who knows.
My clumsy lips shape hymns, invitations

to a place I can't climb back to.
Against the church wall, not singing,
a blind man stands alone
with outstretched hands
on which rain starts to spit.

10 Envoi

The engine throbs;
the island
already
foreign.

The runway
a dark finger
flicking me up,
out to sea.

WOMEN WALKING

My day is fettered by my mother's steps.
I learn the shopping list by heart,
discover architraves.
Walking this slowly
I nearly lose my balance.
I've not got that long—
at my pace I'd be going
somewhere, not marking time,
her arm locked on to mine.

*

My daughter's somewhere else.
Her tenseness fusses me
into unsteadiness.
Her arm is wooden.
Once there was suppleness,
a give and take,
a comfortable distance.
I didn't ask for this—
time, pace, speed, out of my hands.

*

Haven't we walked this way before
—a child fumbling, breathless,
clutching to keep up;
a mother tethered to a clinging hand?

DAY TRIP

Two women, seventies, hold hands
on the edge of Essex,
hair in strong nets,
shrieked laughter echoing gulls
as shingle sucks from under feet
easing in brine.

There must be an unspoken point
when the sea feels like
their future. No longer paddling,
ankles submerge in lace,
in satin ripple.
Dress hems darken.

They do not risk their balance
for the shimmering of ships
at the horizon's sweep
as, thigh deep, they inch on
fingers splayed, wrists bent,
learning to walk again.

CURTAINS

Crocheted
they censored light,
grudging flowers
stippled on the wall.

Warped hems
sealed in silence,
empty formalities
of clocks.

Steeped in vinegar,
bleached too decent
for pity or contempt,
they were veils

knotted
against curiosity,
worn enemies
of easy come and go

though cold forced entry,
its fingers
tarnishing every surface
of the room.

Perhaps they were
nourished
by the salt vapours
of her misery:

after she'd gone
their patterns
crumbled
in our hands.

FAMILY PLANNING

Here is my clutch of humbugs, fickle honey-bees
swarming, sedate. Pleased to see me
—aren't you, my fondant fancies?
I want you filling every hollow of my house;
I need more. More.
Another journey to the suburbs.

I wait till after midnight,
watch bedroom lights shut off, slip
down side passages, over well-clipped lawns
searching for them. Plucking them from walls
and window sills, I tickle their ears
with tales of fish heads, drop them in my basket,
close the lid. You welcome strangers coolly
my wasps, my soft moss-agates.

I have founded a dynasty. If these pharaohs
quarrel, they turn into racoons,
tails fat with malice; I croon them
into sulky tolerance. As it grows dark
they seethe across the flagstones;
a hundred phosphorescent pools
spangle the night courtyard, pitiless.
Hunt well, my predatory loves.

At dawn the kitchen air is heavy,
moist with cat breath; on the range
the mound heaves gently,
until the hot ones struggle from beneath,
clamber on top—as, had I married,
my children might have played hand sandwiches.

VERTIGO

If I should start to think too vividly
of how, while I lie here, tossing for rest,
enduring night, you, earthed at a different angle,
sit on a pine-clad hill, miles to the west

and paint the sun in wine, gaze out at peaks
adorned by ancient names; or, drunk with talk
of old times with old friends becoming old,
circle your finger with a whiskered stalk

of Rocky Mountain poppy, I should lose
my balance, slide to childhood make-believe,
step off the world's edge, plummet, fly apart
and carried, senseless, in the wind's wide sleeve,

atoms of me might fall in foreign rain
defying odds, in touch with you again.

MIRACLE IN THE SEA OF GALILEE

In pampered pilgrimage
we drive, following the map,
to Galilee. Town-soft,
our feet are bruised by stones
until, deep water lifting us,
we strike out, separate.

The water's chill under its skin
so we are vigorous.
Flight of your white arm
extending on the edge of vision.
I turn to you, flip away;
Mount Tabor seems less distant.

Returning to shallows I lie still,
nuzzled by fish,
sun comforting my shoulders;
fish babies, mother-tied invisibly,
risk jerky, brief adventures
among flecked stones.

I collect *famille rose*
—spectrum of flesh pigments,
shapes sugared-almond smooth.
Pinks fine-veined as petals,
pale orange glisten of roe, terracotta,
burnt umber: colours born in water.

Suppose we should turn into pebbles
coloured like earth
baked hard, fire-simplified,
and lose all angularities
in the ebb and flood,
pain-free, indifferent . . .

My fingers close on something conical.
I look up, find you near;
we open our hands
in yours, as in mine,
out of a million stones,
a tiny, living shell.

LETTER FROM SZECHUAN

You cannot prevent the birds of sorrow flying over your head,
but you can prevent them building nests in your hair.

(Chinese proverb)

Wisdom of fools and schoolmasters
—men whose heads are cabinets of drawers,
contents wax-sealed.
No purchase there for birds;
claws, sliding over perfect lacquer,
rattle the handles, bring, for a moment only,
a flutter to the dark interiors.

But we are made differently, Yi Lin.
If I could tell you of the birds,
how they have settled with me
since you were taken,
I know you would say, 'And I, and I!'
Let me write as if . . .

That first morning, having slept at last,
I woke to a jostle of high notes.
I felt their weight, talons
grasping loops of hair,
twisting for footholds, already tangling
strands into a nest;
crying—a narrow song,
without resolution.

I have learned their ways.
Though I cannot see them, I know
they are the colours of tarnish,
eggs heavy, leather-surfaced, rough.
They are dim-witted rather than malevolent
—pecking through my skull, not seeing
that when they have devoured hope, memory,
they will be homeless.

Birds of happiness have many songs,
these only one—my friend,
in whatever province you are lying
they sing it for you too.

BALANCING ACCOUNTS

She's packed
ready to lose him
at a moment's notice.
Marching orders come
in that slight stammer
she's loved so much
in words she knows already.

She starts to speak.
He glances at the clock,
a habit she's trimmed to.
She draws together
all traces of herself.
She has a train to catch.

Or else

the sense of that bag
waiting, seeking attention,
its silent provocation
like someone
turning the first cheek,
weighs with him increasingly.

He knows her need
for ends tied up,
her inability to wear guilt
gracefully. Generous,
he sends her packing;
only, he'd be undone
by talk.

POPPIES

He used arrive without no warnin'
just phone from somewhere
on the motorway. Hurry, quick
put on fresh sheets
run to Patel's—sausages, white bread
chocolate biscuits
(I think his wife a healthy livin' lady)
grab poppies from the yard
stuff them in a glass
put on dress he say he like once.

Sit and shiver. Afraid I ugly,
afraid his face fall, look aside;
no words—he don't want me
chattin' on, with him a swallow
swoopin' all over on the motorways.
Each time I forget he talk so easy.

Stories! People I never see
dance colours on the empty wall;
he make me laugh like never,
he make the stories loosen in me
only I too shy. It get late
and now poppies droopin', but he not.
He really like me, it me he lookin' at
like it the first time always.
He stroke my face, breasts, like wonder,
soft kiss my lips so they perfect.

That last time he say he love me.
He surprise as me—we both laugh.
He not come again. Ever since,
I dreamin' often I lyin' in the yard
can't move nothin', and my nipples
blossomin' with poppies.

THE UNCERTAINTY OF THE POET

(after de Chirico)

1

Is there no answer to sexual obsession
—humiliation of this clown that won't lie down
but leads me to jump absurd
into unsuitable beds, leaving the Muse unserved?
O cul-de-sac delusions, love sickness
that warps imagination, subverts art.

The Corybantes knew the way of it,
those self-made eunuchs in Cybele's name
—well, my neglected and neglectful Muse,
I'll go to Dayton, Ohio. There they trap
the lecher in the brain, lobotomize . . .
a certain way to end the sabotage.

2

The organ withers, sleeps. My work
will flower—no women squeezing juices
that should be the Muse's. But these breasts
and broadened hips I've grown are disconcerting,
and it hurts when, hugging old friends,
I see myself reflected in their frozen eyes.

Arms, hands are a distraction. I've never doubted
that losing all libido for Her sake
will liberate great verses from my pen.
But when? My fingers ache to stroke warm flesh,
plant trees, shape earthen figures. The first step
made others easier; I'll ring Dayton, Ohio.

3

Without arms, I no longer had to play at respectable
employment. I could embrace (so to speak) the role of poet.
But bureaucrats refused to pension me
while I could walk. I could be a traffic warden,
'pleasant outdoor work'. I'd write tickets with my teeth;
they'd give a tactfully remodelled uniform.

So I've had my legs removed. It was time in any case
—for months I'd been unable to sit still. Each time
I settled at my table—torment; an unappeasable desire
to dance, to walk a tightrope, clamber up rocks,
dabble in foot painting . . . I'm one of their most
rewarding clients they tell me, here in Dayton, Ohio.

4

It's winter. They've given me a room looking out
over the plains, where I can write uninterrupted
on my remote-control word processor. Ideas spin
prosy patterns, images inane as ticker-tape,
streams of dead metaphors. Why is there no spark?
If I asked them to excise the intellect,

all senses, leaving only the heart, could I achieve
sensibility distilled, the perfect poem? Worth the price
of not being able to impart it—except to Her.
The decapitation fee here at Dayton, Ohio,
is extremely high. But I can sell my house,
my books, my—everything. I shan't be needing them.

5

They have positioned me on the terrace. I can feel sun on
my skin, though I am cold. I sense the vibration of a
distant train: the Muse, perhaps, leaving for a more fertile
climate? As my pulse slows, syncopated, I imagine, next to
me, phantasms of poems, clustered, like fruits: gold,
growing vigorously from the central stem. One, broken off

JAMES HARRINGTON'S LAMENT

*(James Harrington, the seventeenth-century political
philosopher, when imprisoned in the Tower, believed that his
sweat was turning into bees)*

New life—out of the swamp of flesh,
emerging damp as swimmers
on a surge of tide, cast up, inert
until a tremor, uncertain singing,
a frither of wings confirms the miracle.

They swell, fill out as apples do
from ruins of limp flowers,
then show their separate power, detached
as apples from the tree—a fellowship
of strangers, no longer needing me.

This fruition would make me glad
but for the whisper of ambition
that this be just the start, that I'll go on
to vomit doves, weep fish,
expel children from my deepest orifice.

For knowing the leap of one becoming two
we punish women. And, not to face our grief,
we chase cold secrets of the galaxy,
plumb oceans, raise spires, shivering at dreams
that make of our greatest doings, clumsy tricks.

THE ARCHBISHOP AND THE CARDINAL

Two old men
stand in the palace garden
in their dressing-up clothes.

Hats architectural
—one a dome, the other
flying buttressed—garments

velvet, watered silk,
loops of gold chain,
these walking oxymorons

wear curious expressions
—as though the Cardinal's
found something more delicious

than the fifth deadly sin
to which his ample chasuble
bears witness.

In Lambeth back-streets
rack-rented tenants
spill on to landings.

In Liverpool
too many children
drive women mad,

while here, two old men
amble on the lawn,
landlord, father by proxy

—though it's not personal.
He might have been
a country schoolmaster

and he, with his
ruddy, potato face,
a labourer.

And these starched linens,
fine worsteds, could stand
empty, gossiping together.

PICTOGRAPH IN DUST

Our land has forgotten the taste of rain,
the sky hot, scorning us for years.
We wander, settle for a time,
build houses round ourselves,
cut doors out last.

White men came on roaring carts,
showed us by signs
a different kind of place
where water leaps out of the earth
and we could live soft always.

But this is where we grew.
We are dry people, deep-rooted as thorns,
baked like our cooking-pots.
The earth holds the shape of our heels;
our ancestors need our songs.

They pointed at the sky,
played frightened, waved their arms,
then shook their heads, went away.
The land threw dust
into the air behind them.

Three dawns. Sky flash. An extra sun,
a monstrous cloud, beautiful as rain-dreams,
blossoming. We lost ourselves in looking,
lost our skin, our hair.
Was this what they were pointing to?

And lately, a new sickness.
The strangeness of it made us weep
until the elders spoke:
'All death is one,
only the tracks we take to it are different.'

Could we scratch pictures,
tell people who come after us, and after,
how the white men's spirits are terrible
to those who raise their eyes
above the thorns?

We are building our last houses
—as we have always built
but with no doors. We shall grow light,
crumble like earthenware,
become the land.

GOING UP THE LINE: FLANDERS

Mme Verklaede, mother of four tall sons,
hangs out washing on a fine drying day,
shirt after shirt facing the same way,
off on their anchored dance.

One, swollen with bravado,
advances towards the sky;
another writhes, reluctant to yield
to the sun's shifty blandishments.
This tattered one, a plaything for the cat,
draggles its limp sleeve along the grass.
While that one hangs crucified,
its striped brother, made of different stuff,
clowns in frantic acrobatics.
Another catches its hem on rose-thorns,
resists the summons of the wind
that makes its neighbours chatter.

Here, from beneath our feet
—were there an instrument patient enough
to tease messages along the threads—
we could exhume the uniforms,
scrape off mud, tip out the bones,
reconstitute the men who hung on them.
The biography of one nineteen-year-old
would stretch for miles
telling how he shivered that July,
played cards, wrote half-truths home,
clutched a frail talisman inside his tunic,
faint with heart-beats louder than the shells.

Mme Verklaede starts to gather up
and fold her wind-threshed harvest.
A calm evening; a faint breeze from the West
carries the bugle: the last post, from Ypres.

WAR PHOTOGRAPHER

The reassurance of the frame is flexible
—you can think that just outside it
people eat, sleep, love normally
while I seek out the tragic, the absurd,
to make a subject.
Or if the picture's such as lifts the heart
the firmness of the edges can convince you
this is how things are

—as when at Ascot once
I took a pair of peach, sun-gilded girls
rolling, silk-crumpled, on the grass
in champagne giggles

—as last week, when I followed a small girl
staggering down some devastated street,
hip thrust out under a baby's weight.
She saw me seeing her; my finger pressed.

At the corner, the first bomb of the morning
shattered the stones.
Instinct prevailing, she dropped her burden
and, mouth too small for her dark scream,
began to run . . .

The picture showed the little mother
the almost-smile. Their caption read
'Even in hell the human spirit
triumphs over all.'
But hell, like heaven, is untidy,
its boundaries
arbitrary as a blood stain on a wall.

GRAFFITI

Paper having acquired a poor image,
they each in turn took a diamond stylus,
signed the treaty on a sheet of glass,
words clear against a background of red or blue.

They posed for the cameras, hair lacquered,
identical suits, each middle button fastened
to conceal the rate of respiration
and prevent any unplanned flapping of the tie.

They shook hands in ritually prescribed order,
crossing fingers in left trouser pockets
to neutralize untruth. Smiles locked in place
they saw the blood in one another's eyes.

They put on their spectacles, made speeches
(mutually incomprehensible, all equally sincere)
broadcast to the world
a sense of their historic destiny.

Then they flew home, unbuttoning their suits.
One had inscribed his name in mirror-writing.
Later, when the treaty was overturned,
he was found to be the only one on the right side.

CHANGING THE SUBJECT

DRIVING THROUGH FRANCE

Between croissants and croque monsieur,
in the time it takes Madame Du Plessis
to wash her coffee bowl,
take up her basket
and walk down to the shops and back,
greeting her neighbours occasionally

we have covered 174 kilometres,
passed through 23 villages
in which 237 women, 84 men and 30 dogs
were walking to the shops, or back
—and have not moved,
nor greeted anyone.

*

When I was about eight, I thought
what luck that I was born
English—not foreign
like most people in the world.

Now, flashing through yet another
undistinguished village, it strikes me
that, for some, the centre of the world
is this strip of houses called Rièstard;

whereas I know it is London
or, rather, Crouch End
or, currently,
this Ford Fiesta.

*

Here are three images:
a round bed of sunflowers in a wheat-field;
an albino boy leaning on a wall;
a pair of gates shaped like swans embracing.

Perhaps it wasn't really a flower-bed,
nor the boy really albino, nor the gates
the shape of swans. Perhaps
speed made them remarkable.

I can't return them.
I could embroider them to arbitrary life;
or file them, tokens that something happened,
like the programme from the *son et lumière*.

ON NOT BEING A NATURE POET

Picking up a small, white feather
I note its symmetry, each tiny rib
knowing its proper measure.

I hold it in my palm, and speculate
how many I would have to balance there
before I'd feel the weight.

I see its consummate design, spare
curve like a careful hand, repelling water,
nurturing warm air.

Stroking along its spine, I like to sense
the finger-numbing softness near the root
change to resilience.

But it doesn't move me; I can't say
I love it. As I've written this, the wind
has carried it away.

STRAWBERRIES

I'm spun through time widdershins
to a room lumbered
with a childhood's furniture:
stout mahogany, teak that ousted it,
boxy armchairs, brocatelle
that smartened them as my parents
more or less kept pace with progress
—all there, sharing head-space,
colours mixed by memory to a common brown,

though outside, through French windows,
stand the well-mannered, dusty greens
of a town garden—where I hear
heels clack along the path: my mother
back from a hundred shopping trips
with some treat tucked into her basket;
and where I see my father, the day
he ran to buy me strawberries
and found it was a rag-and-bone man.

As she comes, my vague unease dissolves
—home will be home again;
and, as he does, the wrench
of wishing I could open up his hand,
show him a treat he didn't know he'd brought.

SHOWING

We brought our mothers' photos in
and had a show. We propped them
in a row along a shelf,
scrutinized their conformation:

Christine's, who went out to work
and voted Labour
—a straight-backed Scottish terrier,
tough and guarded.

Mrs Ascoli's borzoi profile
—taut nerves and tragedy;
exquisite in pearls and flowered straw,
head angled in the subtlest condescension.

Mary's, old and sad
—a bloodhound, hair in loops.
Jane's stocky, cheerful pug-dog of a mother
four-square with a golf-club.

Only mine was human
—a musical-box dancer
radiant in a thousand sequins.
They all agreed she was the prettiest.

Then I was ashamed I'd brought that one
—she and my father at the Ladies' Night,
eyes shining at each other;
the one that looked like history.

BIRTH RITE

Since I've not known another birth
this surgery seems natural.
I've left my home
and have come here
to be prepared.

You are my grail
and I must purify myself
—be stripped, shaved, emptied,
wrapped in white—
before I gain you.

Soon you'll be lifted
from the domain of wishes
and we who have been so intimate
will touch at last. Perhaps
we'll be awkward with each other.

Hiss of trolley wheels,
haze of lights . . . I'm drawn
through deepest passages,
protected, raised; someone
holds my hand perfectly.

To be reborn with you
I shed responsibility,
my social face,
speech, consciousness.
I reach back to the dark.

MOTHER'S DAY

for Phyllida Barlow Peake

'You don't care! They always die!
You're never any good with animals.'
Slammed doors,
a storm of tears
gusting up the road to school.

In the still kitchen,
fine-boned Topsy
back from her caesarian,
lies with her surviving kitten,
both too drugged to feed.

It fits my hand,
palpitating, so light.
I stare out at the sooty garden,
cemetery for gerbils, budgies, rabbits,
all my miscarriages of love.

Too much to do.
The spiteful ticking of the clock
reminds me—each day
a fight against chaos,
barely won.

But now I'm on my knees.
My fingers try to be a mother's tongue,
roughing it awake.
It stirs. I clamp
its mouth around her teat.

Its head lolls slack.
I'm hectoring them now,
almost angry at their
easiness with death.
All day, I will them, all day

I'm forcing them together.
The house suspends its breath.
My breasts tingle with desire
for this connection.
And then, it's finished

—mother and baby locked,
Topsy licking, purring.
Here, on my lap,
to weigh against a dozen graves,
this tiny Lazarus.

LADY WILDE TAKES LEAVE
OF HER CRITICS

'Lasciate ogni speranza voi ch'entrate'

Now it has come to this—it's easy
for you to shun me, tittering
behind your hands—yet you know
I am descended from Dante Alighieri.

You've seen me when I was
magnificent—crowned with laurel,
attended by my sons. All Dublin,
London, sought my hospitality

—my salon was the birthplace
of ideas. We all had genius.
The world that mattered—Browning,
Ruskin, Yeats . . . they all came.

There were no petty differences
of sex or race. Contemptuous
of fashion, I was my own creation,
cheating time with artificial dusk.

I don't give house-room to regret.
I chose the pseudonym 'Speranza'
to live my life by, never looked
for squalor. Now, again, it drags at me:

this great misfortune. You may keep
your purblind pity; my grief
is not for your narrow reasons
—I was always above respectability—

it is because he's so diminished.
I never thought. . . he cannot seem
to turn disgrace to his own ends,
laugh at it, knowing he is immortal.

I try to breathe courage into him
but I've drawn on hope too heavily.
He is an oyster, shell torn away.
I am an empty carapace.

WOMAN BATHING IN A STREAM:
Rembrandt

Just 'woman'.
We know it was your Hendrickje,
who bore your daughter,
reared your son,
fed you, clothed and sheltered you,
sat, stood, lay down for you,
and who, even in death,
kept you from creditors.
Almost everything we know of her
is what she did for you.

I'm angry for her
—that you took everything,
made her a vehicle for light,
shadow and reflection
and gave her only anonymity
—as now, in fashion photographs:
dress by Cardin,
hat by David Shilling,
ear-rings, necklace by Adrian Mann
and a model with no name.

Yet I can see how you refused to prettify
the ungainly shift, hoisted to hip level,
thick thighs, peasant forearms, shoulders;
how you seem to have felt their balance,
understood her spirit weight
—painted almost in her idiom.
She must have known—no wonder, then,
the serene half-smile, lack of artifice.
Being so recognized
perhaps made simple fame irrelevant.

THE BALCONY: after Manet

We form a perfect composition,
a triangle, he at the apex;
soft, glutton's hands
smelling of sandalwood and Havanas.
Though I gaze down at the street,
I know how his thumb and index finger
stroke each other, round and round,
oh, so slowly.
A woman's skin: a sheaf of banknotes.

I dig my fingers hard against my fan
to block the screaming.
I could gather up my skirts
and vault the rail;
or leap at him, plunge my nails
into those too easy going eyes.
But I sit here,
tame as this agapanthus in a pot,
central, yet marginal.

My little sister with the holy look
falters on the threshold. Will she
step on to the balcony beside me,
her cachou breath warm on my cheek?
Or will she stay, give him
that second's sweet complicity
for which he waits,
a faint flush rising,
stroking, stroking?

GIRLS AWAKE, ASLEEP

Young girls up all hours
devouring time-is-money on the phone:
conspiracies of mirth,
sharp analyses of friends' defects,
confession, slander, speculation
—all the little mundane bravenesses
that press the boundaries
of what can be thought, felt and talked about.
Their clear-voiced punctuation rings
up stair-wells, to where parents toss
and groan, a sense of their own tolerance
some consolation for short nights, long bills.

Young girls in bed all hours
fathom sleep oceans,
drink oblivion with their deep breaths,
suck it like milk.
Curled round their own warmth,
they fat-cat on the cream of sleep
lapping dreams.
For this, they will resist all calling.
Surfing the crests of feather billows
they ride some sleek dream animal,
pulling the silk strands of his mane,
urging him on.

PICCADILLY LINE

Girls, dressed for dancing,
board the tube at Earl's Court,
flutter, settle.
Chattering, excited by a vision
of glitter, their fragile bodies
carry invisible antennae,
missing nothing.
Faces velvet with bright camouflage,
they're unsung stars—so young
it's thrilling just to be away from home.

One shrieks, points, springs away.
She's seen a moth
caught up in the blonde strands
of her companion's hair,
a moth, marked
with all the shadow colours of blonde.
The friend's not scared;
gently, she shakes her head,
tumbles it, dead,
into her hands.

At Piccadilly Circus they take flight,
skim the escalator,
brush past the collector,
up to the lure of light.

CHANGING THE SUBJECT

1 *The Word*

It started with my grandmother
who, fading unspeakably,
lay in the blue room; disappeared
leaving a cardboard box,
coils of chalky-brown rubber tube.

I inherited her room, her key.
The walls were papered bright
but the unsayable word
seeped through; some nights
I heard it in the dripping of the tap.

I saw it in my parents' mouths,
how it twisted lips for whispers
before they changed the subject.
I saw it through fingers
screening me from news.

The word has rooted in my head
casting blue shadows.
It has put on flesh,
spawned strong and crazy children
who wake, reach out their claws.

2 *Out-Patients*

Women stripped to the waist,
wrapped in blue,
we are a uniform edition
waiting to be read.

These plain covers suit us:
we're inexplicit,
it's not our style to advertise
our fearful narratives.

My turn. He reads my breasts
like braille, finding the lump
I knew was there. This is
the episode I could see coming

—although he's reassuring,
doesn't think it's sinister
but just to be quite clear . . .
He's taking over,

he'll be the writer now,
the plot-master,
and I must wait
to read my next instalment.

3 *Diagnosis*

He was good at telling,
gentle, but direct;
he stayed with me
while I recovered breath,
started to collect

stumbling questions. He said
cancer with a small c
  —the raw stuff of routine—
yet his manner showed
he knew it couldn't be ordinary for me.

Walking down the road
I shivered like a gong
that's just been struck
—mutilation . . . what have I done . . .
my child . . . how long . . .

—and noticed how
the vast possible array
of individual speech
is whittled by bad news
to what all frightened people say.

That night, the freak storm.
I listened to trees fall,
stout fences crack,
felt the house shudder as the wind
howled the truest cliché of them all.

4 *In-Patient*

I have inherited another woman's flowers.
She's left no after-scent, fallen hairs,
no echoes of her voice,
no sign of who or how she was

or through which door she made her exit.
Only these bouquets—carnations,
tiger lilies, hothouse roses,
meretricious everlasting flowers.

By day, they form the set in which I play
the patient—one of a long line
of actresses who've played the part
on this small white stage.

It's a script rich in alternatives.
Each reading reveals something new,
so I perform variously—not falsehoods,
just the interpretations I can manage.

At night, the flowers are oracles.
Sometimes they seem to promise a long run;
then frighten me with their bowing heads,
their hint of swan-songs.

5 *Woman in Pink*

The big, beautiful copper-haired
woman in the next bed
is drowning in pink.

She wears pink frills,
pink fluffy cardigan and slippers.
Her 'get well' cards carry pink messages.

Her husband brings pink tissues,
a pink china kitten; he pats her head.
She speaks in a pink powder voice.

Yet she is big and beautiful and coppery.
At night, she cries bitterly,
coughs and coughs from her broad chest.

They've done all they can.
She's taking home bottles of morphine syrup,
its colour indeterminate.

6 *How Are You?*

When he asked me that
what if I'd said,
rather than 'very well',
'dreadful—full of dread'?

Since I have known this,
language has cracked,
meanings have re-arranged;
dream, risk and fact

changed places. Tenses tip,
word-roots are suddenly
important, some grip
on the slippery.

We're on thin linguistic ice
lifelong, but I see through;
I read the sentence
we are all subject to

in the stopped mouths of those
who once were 'I',
full-fleshed, confident
using the verb 'to die'

of plants and pets and parents
until the immense
contingency of things
deleted sense.

They are his future
as well as mine,
but I won't make him look.
I say, 'I'm fine'.

7 Anna

Visiting time. Anna rises from her bed,
walks down the ward, slowly,
treading glass. She wears
her hand-sewn patchwork dressing-gown,
cut full, concealing her swollen abdomen.

She smiles at people she passes;
pulls her shoulders back,
making a joke about deportment;
waves a skeletal hand
at Mrs Shah, who speaks no English.

Her little girls sit by her bed
in their school uniforms. Too good,
they're silent as they watch her,
tall in her brave vestment
of patterned tesserae

that once were other garments
—as she was: a patchwork mother
made of innumerable creative acts
which they'll inherit with her robe
and make of them something new.

She stops. We hold our breath.
Gaining time, she whispers to a nurse
then turns, walks back to her children,
smiling. Look, she is telling them,
I'm still familiar. I belong to you.

8 *Knowing Our Place*

Class is irrelevant in here.
We're part of a new scale
—mobility is all one way
and the least respected
are envied most.

First, the benigns,
in for a night or two,
nervous, but unappalled;
foolishly glad their bodies
don't behave like *that*.

Then the exploratories;
can't wait to know, but have to.
Greedy for signs, they swing
from misery to confidence,
or just endure.

The primaries are in
for surgery—what kind? What then?
Shocked, tearful perhaps;
things happening too fast.
Still can't believe it, really.

The reconstructions are survivors,
experienced, detached.
They're bent on being almost normal;
don't want to think
of other possibilities.

Secondaries (treatment)
are often angry—with doctors, fate . . .
—or blame themselves.
They want to tell their stories,
not to feel so alone.

Secondaries (palliative)
are admitted swathed in pain.
They become gentle, grateful,
they've learned to live
one day at a time.

Terminals are royalty,
beyond the rest of us.
They lie in side-rooms
flanked by exhausted relatives,
sans everything.

We learn the social map
fast. Beneath the ordinary chat,
jokes, kindnesses, we're scavengers,
gnawing at each other's histories
for scraps of hope.

9 *Difficult Passages*

'You did not proper practise',
my cello teacher's sorrowful
mid-European vowels reproached me.
'Many times play through the piece
is not the proper practising
—you must repeat difficult passages
so when you make performance
there is no fear—you know
the music is inside your capacity.'
Her stabbing finger, moist gaze,
sought to plant the lesson in my soul.

I've practised pain for forty years
—all those Chinese burns;
the home-made dynamo we used
to test our tolerance for shocks;
hands wrapped round snowballs;
untreated corns—all pain practice.
Fine—if I can choose the repertoire.
But what if some day I'm required
to play a great pain concerto?
Will that be inside my capacity?

10 *Outside*

I've hung the washing out
and turn to see
the door slammed shut
by a capricious wind.

Locked out, face to the glass,
I see myself reflected
in the mirror opposite,
framed, slightly menacing.

No need for wuthering
to feel how it might be
—I have that sepia, far-seeing
look of long-dead people.

Perhaps I wouldn't feel dead,
just confused, lost track of time;
could it be years since I turned
with that mouthful of pegs?

And might I now beat on the glass
with jelly fists, my breath
making no cloud in this crisp air,
shout with no sound coming?

Death could seem this accidental
—the play of cells
mad as the freakishness of weather,
the arbitrary shutting out.

Might there be some self left
to look back, register
the shape of the receding house?
And would it feel this cold?

11 *Choosing the Furniture*

The curtains said:
what do you fear more than anything?
Look at it now.

A white room.
I lie and cannot speak,
can not get up.
I stream with pain from every part.
I cry, scream until the sound chokes me.
Someone at the door looks in,
glances at her watch, moves on.
No one comes. No one
will ever come.

The lamp said:
think of what would be most blissful
—what do you see?

A white room
lined with books; a window
looking out on trees and water;
bright rugs, a couch, a huge table
where I sit, words spinning from my fingers.
No one comes; time is limitless,
alone is perfect.
Someone leaves food at the gate
—fruit, bread, little chocolate birds.

The moon laughed:
there is only one room.
You choose the furniture.

12 *I Shall Paint My Nails Red*

Because a bit of colour is a public service.

Because I am proud of my hands.

Because it will remind me I'm a woman.

Because I will look like a survivor.

Because I can admire them in traffic jams.

Because my daughter will say ugh.

Because my lover will be surprised.

Because it is quicker than dyeing my hair.

Because it is a ten-minute moratorium.

Because it is reversible.

In my fiftieth year,
with my folded chin
that makes my daughter call me Touché Turtle;

in my fiftieth year,
with a brood of half-tamed fears
clinging around my hem,

I sit with my green shiny notebook
and my battered red notebook
and my notebook with the marbled cover,

and I want to feel
revolutions spinning me apart,
re-forming me

—as would be fitting in one's fiftieth year.

Instead, I hum a tune to my own pulse.

Instead, I busy dead flies off the sill
and realign my dictionaries.

Instead, through the window,
I make a sign of solidarity
at swallows, massing along the wires.

VISITING DUNCAN

for Nancy Stepan

I'm on a day trip to our shared frontier,
pass tissue-wrapped daffodils, chocolate
across the gap; my greeting warm, but careful,
taking the measure of your foreignness.
How far have you travelled

in your migration to that other country
whose landscape, customs, I can only guess?
It's an America, dividing you from me
by language much like mine, yet skewed,
stripped. I make conversation:

'Nurse says you went to Hastings yesterday
—I wonder if you remember . . .'
'Was it meant to be memorable?' you ask,
not meaning, I think, to be witty
though later I'll laugh, remembering.

You don't talk about the old country,
little of the new—as you did once
when contrast, loss, were everything.
The discourse you've learned here
is that of emptiness.

You examine the dimensions of the void
with all your old precision; picking up
a letter from your son, 'Do I miss him?
What would be the test? Do I wish
he were here? I think not.'

A woman comes into your room. 'I have
nothing', she says. Just that, twice,
and leaves. Later, another: 'I'm so hungry
—can you give me food . . . nothing all day.'
You break her off some chocolate.

'It's an existence'. You leave
the alternative unsaid. Your final exile
has no reference points; in an hour
you won't know I was here. There's only now;
this only kiss; these hands, holding.

THE BED

When they were young, and she a captive
in her parents' house, he'd climb
in through her window. They'd whisper,
touch, slip together in her narrow bed
until the rooster pulled them separate
and sent him, singing, to the field.

Their marriage bed was ample.
Child after child was born in it
until, pushed to the side, he played
the hero in the field, the tavern.
Resentments multiplied; the bed was
for sleeping, back towards back, alone.

In middle age, as she gained flesh,
he lightened, rolled towards the centre.
One night, he floated from his dream,
found her arm curved around him,
hand tucked under his side,
and she was murmuring an old song.

In their seventies, he took a saw,
halved the bed's width. Climbing in
earlier each day, they found
a dozen different ways of fitting,
fusing at last into a shape so right
they felt no further need to move apart.

RUBY WEDDING

Forty years this month
since you hurtled round the corner
into me, taking my breath away.

Eye-watering you were
like lemons after long thirst,
a burst of bubbles.

I'd learned to patch my emptiness
with tidy habits,
was comforted by order,

but you—a bouquet of astonishments
a chaos I fought
then learned to mingle with.

Sometimes I'd watch you sleeping,
switchback your breath—even then
you seemed so vivid.

I'd rub your hands
skin turning to plastic, paper,
then to ash.

As I've cleared
your squirrelled papers, ornaments,
order has ticked back into every room.

I have been slow
to cast off from the bed
in which we joined and parted

but now I'm drifting out.
You have breathed my last breath.
My heart is jumping for the two of us.

PARTNERS

It was always said—she
was the strong one,
the emphasis implying
something not quite natural.

It showed in her head's angle
inherited from a line of officers
khaki-convincing in the gallery
of family photographs.

She always knew her mind.
He never could decide on anything.
After he died, people said
she'd grown to look like him,

—as if his soul, lacking direction,
had managed a short hop
and settled in that softening jaw,
that bewilderment behind the eyes.

FÜR THERESE

I'll tell you why—

You must understand, since he died
he has that special unreality
that greatness gives; as if he's been distilled
into his Ode to Joy, his Grosse Fuge.

I knew a different man—an embarrassment
to good society, gauche beyond belief!
Tone-poet he may have been, but blind
to the shadow of reproof in Father's eye
—he would hold forth about that Bonaparte.
Almost a child—he'd know he'd caused offence
but not know how, nor how to put it right.

And yet, he altered when we were alone.
He loved me, and I felt for once
powerful—great temptation to a girl
expected to transform from father's daughter
into husband's wife. But then I saw
how we'd grow disappointed with each other
—he with my limited capacity
to understand his art; I with his constant
absence in a world that shut me out.

Frau van Beethoven! Now I'm facing death
I sometimes whisper to myself that title,
missed, and wonder if I could have learned
enough to follow him . . . but after all
our names were not intended to be linked
—even the little piece he wrote for me
that might have been my mark on history,
his publisher misread as *Für Elise*.

NIGHT HARVEST

for Martin

We dredge these small fry
from our separate pools of sleep,
spread them before each other

and sort them, puzzling,
smiling to discover
our several selves in them.

Under water their colours
were subtly different.
Some slipped back as we lifted them

but these are enough, prismatic,
splitting the past, the future
into bright fragments.

We can afford to be extravagant,
throw back the catch,
know it will multiply.

WHY I LIE IN THIS PLACE

We were close once.
I knew him better than I knew myself
—the way his lips tensed when he was moved,
his knack with children,
the smell of his sweat mingled with the horses'
after a fast ride together.

I made no secret of it.
I heard the envious sniggering,
but I sought him out, and he, me,
I swear it. We drank and whored together.
We discussed court business,
talked sport and strategy

—until he changed. In such little ways
at first, mere moments of distraction,
the smile a shade less warm—I didn't think.
And then, as I was talking once, I caught
a glance, thrown by him to his equerry,
as if to say 'that's typical, you see'

and the world somersaulted—suddenly
no longer partner, fellow-witness,
but object, irreversibly split off.
I left the city then, grew hard.
Indifferent to death, I flourished
in far-flung campaigns.

The people sought me out, asked me
to lead the revolt against him. I'd heard
he had become cruel, a voluptuary, oppressive
—they had real grievances. And yet
their quarrel wasn't mine. Had it not been
for that flick of the eyelid

—the hinge on which hung
love and hate, peace and war, the fate
of princedoms and ten thousand little lives—
I'd have bent my strength to his;
what followed would have happened differently.
As it was, I used the masses' anger.

Or was it the reverse?
Perhaps the swell of history
would have rolled on without my part in it.
I only know, but for that look,
these many hundred years,
I should have been lying next to him.

THE CHAIRMAN'S BIRTHDAY

The day before, my father
had visited the butcher's shop himself
to choose the calf's head.

Our pastry cook was gone
(I hadn't thought of him as an Enemy)
so the dessert course would be ordinary.
But the calf's head! Father's speciality.

He held it up to admire its whiteness;
I shunned its eyes, its open baby mouth.
He plunged it in the bubbling pan
covered closely with a piece of cloth
to stop it turning black.

Meanwhile the sauce—Madeira demi-glace—
quenelles of minced truffles,
sautéed cocks' combs . . .

and when the head was lifted steaming,
placed on a platter, he surrounded it
with mushrooms, halves of hard-boiled egg,
sweetbreads, its own sliced tongue and brains,
poured on the sauce, carried it, glistening,
ceremoniously to table.

Because they took him two days later
that evening runs on a continuous reel
inside my head; a melodrama lit by Eisenstein.

Under the chandeliers
Father walks, bearing the dish,
to comic tuba music—though then
it seemed triumphal, dignified.

Cut to the Chairman, who shifts his eyes
as he thanks Father for the feast
while quavering violins,
my father's sweating, deferential forehead,
seem to interrogate the future
and find their own reply.

And then the epilogue
—because I've wondered ever since
if he had slaughtered me,
served me with miraculous garnishes,
would he be living now?

GHOST STATIONS

We are the inheritors. We hide here
at the roots of the perverted city
waiting, practising the Pure Way.
Listening to ourselves, each other,
we find the old soiled words won't do;
often we can only dance our meanings.

Deep in the arteries of London, life
is possible—in the forgotten stations:
York Road, St Mary's, Seething Lane . . .
I love the names. Each day, we sing them
like a psalm, a celebration
—Down Street, British Museum, City Road.

We live on waste. After the current's off
we run along tunnels, through sleeping trains,
ahead of the night cleaners. We find chips,
apple cores (the most nutritious part),
dregs of Coke. On good days, we pick up
coins that fit the chocolate machines.

Once I found a whole bag of shopping.
That night we had an iceberg lettuce,
a honeydew melon, tasting of laughter.
And once, an abutilon—its orange
bee-flowers gladdened us for weeks.
Such things are dangerous;

now, to remind ourselves, we read
the newspapers we use as mattresses.
Or gather on the platforms,
witness the trains as they rip past
(our eyes have grown used to the speed).
Almost every known depravity

is acted out on trains—rape, drunkenness,
robbery, fighting, harassment, abuse.
And the subtler forms—intellectual bullying,
contempt, all the varieties of indifference . . .
We've learned to read the faces;
we need to see these things, simply.

The travellers only see their own reflections.
But lately, a few in such despair
they cup their faces to the glass, weeping,
have seen the ghost stations
and though we're always out of sight,
they sense our difference and find their way.

Our numbers are growing, though there are
reverses. Some lose heart, want to leave.
We can't let them—we keep them all
at Brompton Road, carefully guarded,
plotting uselessly, swapping fantasies,
raving of sunlight, mountains or the sea.

One day, we'll climb out, convert the city!
The trains are full of terrible energy;
we only have example, words. But there is
our chant to strengthen us, our hope-names:
Uxbridge Road, King William Street,
South Kentish Town, South Acton, Bull and Bush . . .

STRIKING DISTANCE

THIS MORNING

Creation might have been like this,
early sun stencilling the leaves
of the first ever walnut trees,
and the cows beside them splashes
of caramel, coffee, apricot, vanilla,
drifting as if under water
in breeze-fractured light.

I have the eyes of the academy,
mince the natural world into word-burgers
seasoned with disappointment.
These lovely prelapsarian cows
are a poem, generous in conception,
perfectly achieved, rhythms,
rhyming, untranslatable.

My gaze makes them alien to themselves.
Bashful, they shift their stout elegance,
breathe soft, uneasy huffs, wrestling
with doubt. But as the church clock strikes
seven, twice over, we are between times,
and simply the world's new inhabitants
staring at the other, staring.

WAITING ROOM

It was slippery blind surfaces,
rushing waterways, a distant drum.

It was drifting at anchor, warm
power of stretch and kick.

Sometimes, there was red to dance to,
and songs: mother-sounds without edges.

I'd answer, but nothing came.
My lips were always practising.

A mouth-fit thumb or a toe
would come to console me.

A time of loud words bruising
against each other; then a giddy shock

hurled me against the dim-lit screen,
unharmed, but understanding I didn't have

the temperament for silent suffering,
that this was the moment to

take on gravity, to haul myself
round, and out on a tide of cries.

THE FALL

The rest of your life starts
when a world of snug non-sense
you've not imagined could be otherwise
turns mean, and there you are,
the usual you and getting
smacked for it, not understanding why.

Did you dream rusks, pat-a-cake, the bliss
you summoned when you squeezed your eyes?
Now smiles are weather.
You learn rain-dance and ritual,
slant looks, pent farts,
the cussedness of spoon and fork.

So much forbidden, you never know all
the names for it. You punish your dolls
for their mistakes, and feel quite cheerful;
only sometimes there's a pellet in your mouth
you can't spit out or swallow,
the bitterness of crusts you're stuck with.

PASSED ON

Before, this box contained my mother.
For months she'd sent me out for index cards,
scribbled with a squirrel concentration
while I'd nag at her, seeing strength
drain, ink-blue, from her finger-ends
providing for a string of hard winters
I was trying not to understand.

Only after, opening it, I saw
how she'd rendered herself down from flesh
to paper, alphabetical; there for me
in every way she could anticipate
—*Acupuncture: conditions suited to*
—*Books to read by age twenty-one*
—*Choux pastry: how to make, when to use.*

The cards looked after me. I'd shuffle them
to almost hear her speak. Then, my days
were box-shaped (or was I playing safe?)
for every doubt or choice, a card that fitted
—*Exams: the best revision strategy*
—*Flowers: cut, how to make them last*
—*Greece: the men, what you need to know.*

But then they seemed to shrink. I'd turn them over,
find them blank; the edges furred, mute,
whole areas wrong, or missing. Had she known?
The language pointed to what wasn't said.
I'd add notes of my own, strange beside
her urgent dogmatism, loosening grip
—*infinitives never telling love*
  lust single issue politics when
  don't hopeless careful trust.

On the beach, I built a hollow cairn,
tipped in the cards. Then I let her go.
The smoke rose thin and clear, slowly blurred.
I've kept the box for diaries, like this.

COAT FOR AN UNDERGRADUATE

From Italy, by way of Harrods.
I snatched it from a wealthy tourist,
this perfect coat, size 9–10 years,
wool and cashmere, silk, exquisite detail.
It flared as I revolved it on its hanger,
deep folds embracing light.

We're excited by it—the cut, the cost.
Aren't we both imagining
it will make you, too, perfect,
propel you down the Broad firm-footed,
give you stature,
free all stiffnesses?

On you, the hem dips,
shoulders poke, empty,
top button, unmanageable.
I rage as I pick open seams,
pin, tack, cut, cack-handed,
compromise the marvellous finish.
Your whole life, make do
and never mended enough.

Look—in the country of the possible,
this is a real transformation.
Child-sized you may be, but here is
your come-of-age reflection;
and you're thinking tall
as you drive away in your red car,
green boots, and the perfect enough coat,
swinging, sock-it-to-them, classy blue.

FILE PAST

While his back's turned I slip inside
my pink, fat file,
the cover flopping shut behind me.
It's hot, airless.

I start to chew through layers of forms,
letters, case conference reports,
leaving a hole the size of me.
I get thirsty.

I notice names. Muscles twitch,
remembering—eyelids, anus, fists.
Such a little hand. Put it here.
Love. Aah. Mustn't tell or. Love

I bite through love
and all the other vomit words
—Security, Care, Sharing, Come to terms—
I can only say with a funny accent.

My name is scattered everywhere
but I'm not in this wad of bits,
this People In My World diagram,
Life Story Book (my life, their story).

Here is a girl who glares with my eyes;
weird clothes, greasy hair, my sort of age
—my mother there are almost no names left for.
Ref. file CP 62/103.

YOU MAKE YOUR BED

You make your bed, precisely not to lie on it
but to confine the disorder of the night
in mitred corners, unruffled surfaces.

Morning's already clamouring in your head.
This is a stand against incompetence,
at least one perfectly accomplished act.

All day it's what you've put behind you,
an infant place that, with the dark, draws you
down, and back; an enticing book

whose soft covers you open, slipping into
those quotidian rehearsals—love
and sleep. And dream irresponsibly

until the bell clangs for the next round.
Loath to climb out, you know you should be glad
you can. You make your bed precisely.

SKIN DISTANCE

Can you imagine this?

You're sitting on the tube
opposite a strapping lad, black,
late teens, seventeen stone-ish.
You haven't noticed him particularly
until he fetches out a jar of
baby-food (creamed carrots),
levers the lid off with his teeth,
spoons up large mouthfuls.

Urgently now, he follows
with turkey dinner, banana delight
sunshine breakfast, rice and pears . . .

And you're feeling queasy, seeing
who you are is accidental
and there's only a couple of skins
between being you, and tipping over

into the life of a young, black, male,
seventeen-stone baby-food junkie
who doesn't seem to care who notices
or what they're thinking.

Can you feel the slither of semolina
creeping across your tongue,
your limbs becoming heavier?

TIDE, TURNING

Sliced flat, androgynous,
a child again with all to play for,
I've come here to encounter the sea.

Clownish, she catches me out, slap on the back
no joke—though I laugh
spluttering while she collapses in ripples.

Mother, she rocks me on her slack, dark breast.
She's quickly bored,
spits in my eye, fiddles with my hair.

Lover with a wicked past, her licks
and soft caresses turn to rough trade
throwing me off balance.

I am a fish she'll try to suck
down to her pebble bed; I am a rod
erect as she curls above me.

Too quick for her—I slice across
her oily invitation, and up
through shards of savage light.

She cuffs me to size
with her grey, glass paw
reminding me who was here first

—and will be here, long after
anyone who reckons she's paid off
her debt to the moon.

GIFTS

When I think of her, I see that swift
flick of her hair,
how she'd stroke it, brush it
lowering her head to where the light
sought out the shine.
She called it her gift.

There was a way she lived in music, rare,
like her last illness.
Her keyboard brilliance
was unremarkable to her—as I
might think of speaking;
or of hair.

Perhaps because by then she had begun
to see it fall
to medical heroics,
she loved it more than gifts she'd only lose
when étude, fugue and hair
would be all one.

Or maybe, in the mirror, her eyes met
the aureole,
brighter than she could bear,
of an enormity—so that she fastened
onto her hair's lustre
all value, all regret.

WOMAN IN BROWN

Woman in brown
almost not there at all;
a shadow, shadowless
propped into a chair against the wall;
eyes, semi-breves,
wrists hanging slack:
anaglyptic undersides of leaves.

Imagine her against light—there,
where sun is shafting through the door.
You'd see through skin
to peristalsis, respiration,
the automatic busyness of circulation
—a clock in a deserted house;
action there's no longer reason for.

But for a chance ordering of matter
this woman might have been
me. But she is the one in brown
and I can wrap her up in verse,
drive back to town
as her thoughts leak gently out
to blizzard on the television screen.

PRESENTS FOR DUNCAN

Ten years ago, I could have brought a book
of Gramsci's, say, or Larkin's. You'd have asked
my views on Europe, taken me to look
at a new camellia; maybe we'd have driven
somewhere for a concert—Bach or Bruch.

Even last year, there might have been a walk,
you in a wheelchair, through the ordered grounds
to the pub beyond the gate. Then, you could talk
about the people in old photographs,
and tell a kestrel from a sparrow hawk.

Opportune, that in middle age we're blind
to future selves, will not imagine some
arterial sabotage could make a mind
that rocketed shrink to random sparks
(since entropy's impartially unkind).

Today, as you catch sight of me, you scream
and wail, knowing yourself, in that moment,
lost. Then reaching, parrot-slow, you seem
content to cram your mouth with an old sweetness:
all the world in a chocolate orange cream.

DEATH SPEAKS AFTER THE TONE

What shall I say to you,
your uni-person voice designed to suit
sales-people, colleagues, closest friends, your son?
You must see it won't do

for me, who know you best.
I was there before you knew yourself.
I understand the fluxion of your heart,
its innermost recess.

'I'm not here right now'
—technology leads you to murder sense.
Or is it fear makes you indifferent
to what words say, and how?

If you'd allow me in,
let me speak directly to you, soon
you'd see I am essential to your life,
its spiritual twin.

You think you'll put me off
if you cower behind that amputated voice
there, not there, never there for me.
But I've time enough.

I'll never go away.
I'll be here, pressed against your grille,
smoked glass, net curtain of a voice,
day after day after day.

THE WAY WE LIVE NOW

I'm walking into *La Porchetta*
with Daughter and ex-Husband
when I spot ex-Lover and new woman
sharing a tricolore salad, mozzarella
soaring mouthwards on a single fork.

94

I think I'm going to faint, but instead
stroll across, force an introduction.
She has strong hair, a usurper's handshake
and 'nice to meet you', she says,
dabbing at her cerise pearl lips.

I retreat with grace to where D
and ex-H can report on how ex-L
and companion are arranging their faces.
I play with my spaghetti marinara;
concentrate on other fish.

The man at the next table tells us he's
my ex-husband's ex-lover's ex-husband:
Neil. Over an espresso, he announces
he's rethought his fellow-travelling
with feminism. He seems to want applause.

My ex knows Neil's ex- and current wives
are planning to move in together.
I know my ex-lover's woman is getting
in touch with her Inner Child and is giving
ex-L a hard time. Though not hard enough.

My daughter knows everything.

WHERE ARE YOU?

In this garden, after a day of rain,
a blackbird is taking soundings,
flinging his counter-tenor line
into blue air, to where
an answering cadenza shows
the shape and depth of his own solitude.

Born in South London, inheritors
of brick, smoke, slate, tarmac,
uneasy with pastoral
as hill-billies with high-rise,
my parents called each other
in blackbird language:
my father's interrogative whistle
—'where are you?'
my mother's note, swooping, dutiful
—'here I am'.

There must have slid into the silences
the other questions,
blind, voiceless worms whose weight
cluttered his tongue;
questions I hear as, half a lifetime on,
I eavesdrop on blackbirds.

MOMENT

Driving to meet you,
a scent surfacing
in the mind
—a random pulse
leaping the wrong synapse—

the trace
of another life
—gunpowder, was it,
or hot vanilla—

overturned the furniture
of love,
as a shaft of air
from an opened window
enlarges an over-heated room.

ONE

Those are the worst times.
Not the cold
ghost at my back
when I turn in the small hours;

not the fury with myself
and you when the screwdriver's
wrong and my hand stumbles
and bleeds;

but after I've halved
the last piece of walnut cake,
or marked in the paper
something that would amuse you

or, at the sales, dithered
over whether you'd like
the check or the blue best
—the small ways

I assume you—then
the Oh, like an uppercut.
And look
I'm talking to you.

OUR PEACOCK

He was a gloss on that English garden of roses,
banks of blowsy peonies, clipped box.
Ours, because we were his only audience,
and one of us, at least, wanting him to be
an oracle, to fill the sad silence between us
with a fanful of gorgeous air, a sign
richer than the sun's feeble water-dance.

Chivvied by a dozen bloomered bantams,
he dragged his train sulkily in the dust,
a legendary actor in a fit of temperament;
but turned then and, with a shiver of quills,
displayed his gifts to us, no holding back;
Platonic peacock strutting his stuff, all symmetry,
brilliancies, rank upon rank of exquisite eyes.

It wasn't nothing, that we were sharing this
in an English garden smelling of lavender.
But his cold glance told me there's no beauty,
anywhere, to set against old failures of love.
As we left, he lifted himself high into a tree,
and cried out; his voice, broken glass
tearing the heart out of the afternoon.

OUT OF REACH

Raja . . . puja . . .
a Tamil song,
catchy in a Madras taxi,
seemed, in the space between near-misses,
to connect the driver's torn shirt,
the bullet-proof vest of the State governor,
quilts fitting the humped backs of cattle.

It's gone
leaving only its impression.
Asking in the music shop
I offer *Raja . . . puja . . .*
as a baby mouths urgent syllables
at kindly adults
deaf to the most important thing.

CROSSING THE BORDER

This cake I'm making—
I'd rather do almost anything else
but I need a place for these ingredients.

Elsewhere, another woman risks
a shell-gashed balcony to light a fire.
She guides a baby's thumb into its mouth.

My cake is made of dry and wet elements.
The god of the fleeting moment
blesses them into something new.

She has boiled pasta, a handful
for her family of four; a smear
of mustard. They call it soup.

This cake is made of such plenty
yet it won't rise.
I mean it as an offering

but how can it fit into a time
of bread in the wrong places,
of no—no more—nothing?

If I could, I'd walk with it
across the map of Europe,
over bland pastels, wavering boundaries,

to where she's silent as a man says,
I won't die of death, but of
Love For My City.

*

Children come like sparrows to my table
flight upon flight; cold
fingers grasp the hard edge,
nails scrabbling for grains of salt.

I eat my warm, rich food. Every day
they have a more migrant look.
Above them, the funeral bird
strops a complacent beak.

Sanity would turn time
back on itself, reel the children in,
to stack them
in vast ovarian warehouses, sleeping.

Let their next life be as meadow larks
—their high, clean thatness;
dying just deaths
unfreighted by love, pride, consequence.

STRIKING DISTANCE

Was there one moment when the woman
who's always lived next door turned stranger
to you? In a time of fearful weather
did the way she laughed, or shook out her mats
make you suddenly feel as though
she'd been nursing a dark side to her difference
and bring that word, in a bitter rush
to the back of the throat—*Croat / Muslim /
Serb*—the name, barbed, ripping
its neat solution through common ground?

Or has she acquired an alien patina
day by uneasy day, unnoticed
as fall-out from a remote explosion?
So you don't know quite when you came to think
the way she sits, or ties her scarf,
is just like a Muslim / Serb / Croat;
and she uses their word for water-melon
as usual, but now it's an irritant
you mimic to ugliness in your head,
surprising yourself in a savage pleasure.

Do you sometimes think, she could be you,
the woman who's trying to be invisible?
Do you have to betray those old complicities
—money worries, sick children, men?

Would an open door be too much pain
if the larger bravery is beyond you
(you can't afford the kind of recklessness
that would take, any more than she could);
while your husband is saying you don't understand
those people / Serbs / Muslims / Croats?

One morning, will you ignore her greeting
and think you see a strange twist to her smile
—for how could she not, then, be strange to herself
(this woman who lives nine inches away)
in the inner place where she'd felt she belonged,
which, now, she'll return to obsessively
as a tongue tries to limit a secret sore?
And as they drive her away, will her face
be unfamiliar, her voice, bearable:
a woman crying, from a long way off?

ADVENT IN BRATISLAVA 1992

for Michael Rustin

Ten days to New Year, the fog's cold comfort
paints the square non-commital.
This passes for a market, ramshackle piles
of moist acrylic sweaters, glass baubles.
Children, like children anywhere,
suck chemical lollipops, staring
at the fog-wrapped, festive tree.

To us, from a more electric city,
this is a place in hibernation,
smatterings of light snuffed easily,
shops, cafés, turned inwards, as if refusing
to whore for passing trade, to get the hang
of the bland competence that's ordinary
up river, and points west.

We're plump with bright ideas, but this
is not the season for practicalities.
In the wedding cake Filharmonia,
fin de siècle bourgeois look-alikes,
treading the frayed red carpet, stroll
through the interval; their apparatchik past
tucked under their tongues, dissolving slowly.

THERE WILL COME A TIME

(*from Marina Tsvetaeva*)

There will come a time, lovely creature,
when I shall be for you—a distant trace
lost in the blue pools of your memory.
You will forget my aquiline profile,
forehead wrapped in a halo of cigarette smoke,
the perpetual laugh I use to hoodwink people,
the hundred silver rings on my tireless hand,
this attic crow's-nest, the sublime confusion
of my papers.　　　　You will not remember
how, in a terrible year, raised up by Troubles,
you were little.　　　And I was young.

(November, 1919)

THE TRIAL OF LYMAN ATKINS

Where he lives, they get along without them,
words. Him and his brothers. Just soft names
to coax the heifers out frosty mornings;
gabble, *gabble*, laughter teasing the turkeys;
once a month, greeting folks in the farmstore.

So he opens his empty mouth, and the words
cluster right where the lawyer puts them
I leaned on her face to stop her screaming
—like singing out *Amen*! to please the pastor,
like saying *I'm shit* to escape from the big guys
(words being light and slack as a string bag
shaped to whatever you want them to hold).

Or, being rare and rarely his own,
is it rather that words, once he hears himself speak them,
come to seem weighty and full of the truth?
Does he get to believe, for as long as he's talking,
that a girl screamed and he was the one who stopped her?
Does he imagine the press of her cheekbones?

Of course, in the nature of things, there's no knowing.
What's clear is he only half understands
—though he's learned the trick of seeming to, just by
repeating the words right after a person:
Yes, I waived my rights, and he's grinning
as if he's seeing himself in a motorcade,
while the jurors look grave, scribble on their note-pads
the words that dance round his head like horse-flies.

AMERICA

for Eva Hoffman

That was a haloed sound
the soft, crisp grace of it
held on the lips,
unfolding into space—
America!

We embarked in new clothes,
the plainest. We'd burned
the old, along with our sins,
all complicated, sad relations,
all slant, avaricious things.

Spring, and a following wind.
We almost rejoiced in spewing up
our very linings, as the gale
big-bellied the mainsail,
caked our hair white.

Our thoughts flew forwards,
singing. Had I understood
there is no innocence
like that of a long journey,
I might have dreaded landfall.

America—raccoon, cardinals,
new colours in the earth.
We trekked through summer,
guided to the place
we called Redemption.

All our wants were wants
for all of us. We were re-made
by daily quartering of bread;
scars, callouses in common.
We were perfected. Prospered . . .

Hard to say in whose bones
the seed of Self had lain like
tubercle. Slowly, we've sickened,
and with diseases one can't name
except by absence.

Our lips are flaking
as we creep into familiar rags
we don't acknowledge. We've become
all closed hands, faces, doors.
I can't live with no America.

SISTER SHIP

On 6 March 1987, the passenger ferry, Herald of Free Enterprise,
capsized outside Zeebrugge, with the loss of 193 lives.

1 *Relatives*

More than a month
they've swallowed strange food,
found patience, grateful phrases,
while gales poured havoc over her.

The town's familiar as a lifer's cell.
At night, they lie counting traffic lights,
brands of beer—unconnected things
to keep them even.

Not much to say;
just waiting, walking streets,
the dock, staring out there,
trying to, trying not to picture him.

Waiting for cranes to raise her,
for the sea to give him back
so they can all go home,
so they can sleep.

2 *Divers*

She's come to term,
a monstrous animal
slouched onto one side
for the delivery.

The sea sulks, stands off.
Tugs bob, useless,
while they, like puny midwives,
delve in her cluttered entrails

half-blind, grasping
a thigh, a shoe,
an arm stiff round a pillar,
easing it free,

becoming
instant mortuary professionals,
prepared for the look
of face after face, defaced.

3 *Afterwards*

The duchess came,
gave him a toy,
said, *Brave little boy.*

The prince came,
admired her curls,
said, *Brave little girl.*

The Minister came,
shook his hand,
talked of England.

The pop star came
with a TV van,
said, *Terrible, man!*

Reporters came,
said, *Tell about the horror.*
Look at the camera.

The ambassador came,
the nun and the police,
the doctor and the priest.

But Daddy didn't come,
Mummy didn't come,
his wife didn't come,

her husband didn't come,
their daughter didn't come,
their sons didn't come,

and night has come
like a black stone
in the throat.

4 *Sister Ship*

Months afterwards
we travel in the sister ship,
our luggage stuffed with images
made toy-like by the geometry
of page or screen.

What can we do with them?
We're bit players in a re-take
with an uneventful ending
turning the one before to history;

though you can sense her weight,
her three and more dimensions
as she slides seaward, slowly turns.

5 *Not us*

That evening,
when the shutting of bow doors
was left to enterprise
and enterprise was sleeping,
would it have been like this:

you and I
out on A deck, watching
receding lights
spangle the ink black,
when suddenly

the sky tips
—funny at first—
pressing us on the rail.
I have inflatable armbands
fit them on you

—or do I make
a bowline from my coat-belt—
either way,
as the surface rushes up
we grasp hands, jump, swim.

Or did it list to starboard?
We're thrown backwards
against an iron stair
we cling to, wedge ourselves
waiting for rescue.

Would it have been
like that? you and I
survivors? Always a way
for those who keep their heads,
those with enterprise?

6 *Cafeteria*

This ship is full of empty passengers,
a cargo of consumers. One could think
we are working our passage with our teeth,
biting, chewing, swallowing our way
from shore to shore.

                 The cafeteria
fills up at once, a patient, silent queue
intent on breakfast: piles of sausages,
tomatoes, baked beans, bacon, eggs, fried bread
and toast and marmalade;

                         as though we've been
invaded by those taken by the sea,
ravenous spirits thrown up in the wake.
We glut ourselves to fill a double void
with obvious comforts, never quite enough.

7 *Anniversary*

They look pinched by a wind
stronger than then
and colder.

They're quiet as they queue
to scatter wreaths and posies
on the water,

shifty sea
that swallowed flesh
as if entitled.

So much salt
our cheeks are stiff with it.

So much salt
our eyes are glazed with it.

The wind spits back
their tears for kin
man–slaughtered,

not mattering enough;
and no one saying sorry.
They're here as witnesses

for those more than fractions
of the one–nine–three,
the paper dead.

So much salt
our stomachs sicken of it.

So much salt
our tongues are raw with it.

They twist their grief into
flowers, cast them adrift.
Anger, more difficult to place.

TURNING POINT

You're standing in the supermarket queue
dreaming of difference;
or on a foreign street, you're weak
with possibilities there's no language for.
And you could walk
round the corner into that other place

but for the hours looping on themselves,
ordinary as knitting
you're too meshed in to see straight.
Each morning dazzles you with a tranche
of choices, distracting
from the sly way the needles skewer you.

Bad faith isn't high dramatic acts
—the Judas kiss, embezzlement—
it's allowing each innocuous stitch
to shift you from day to night
and back to day, no further on,
a little fitter for the shapeless droop

that lengthens to the final
casting off.
Out of what despair, or resolution,
might you refuse? And what
would guide you through
the chaos of your fraying ends?

CUTTING LOOSE

At one time
at moments when the walls burst through the wallpaper
he could pause long enough
to slam the door behind him as he fled
into the hard-boiled street;
so that coming home, hours later, all was intact
—walls, clock, kettle
subdued to simple ticks and shrieks and silences.

Now the door stands gaping
as he hurtles out, in sight of the street's main chancers
and he knows his room will be
picked clean and pissed on (though not with particular malice).
But it seems immaterial,
a room in a film—and the thought is a sudden joy
and a clarification:
instead of a loop, his route will be straight forward.

His feet make jet-streams.
He rides in the bowl of his pelvis like a millionaire
and he sheds desire
for the squared-up scraps of lives in the lighted windows
as his leg-springs carry him
through streets speckled with the whites of eyes,
past Coke can and condom,
the newsprint beds of the rootless, birthday-less,

to the waste-ground
where gaunt backs of warehouses stand, guarded
by hogweed and sycamore.
And though he knows he's matter out of place,
a kind of dirt,
he's a giant under the sky, chewing nettles
like cheekfuls of bliss;
for now, breathing easily, at home.

LIFE IN TALL HOUSES

So many years of the tall, smart
Happy Family museums
insulting us by their indifference to blinds;

blazing rooms, boasting
amply laid tables, modish clutter,
children playing chamber music;

bait, perhaps.

Years of impregnable locks
until we came to imagine more intensely
those hugs, those conservatory flowers;

and the tall houses
cracked open like pomegranates
under the arithmetic of our desire;

a bit too easily.

The people sprang from their beds
with a curdled look, as though we
were what they'd always dreaded and needed.

The light inside the tall houses seems
misplaced, furniture paper-frail,
jasmine bent on dying.

We are left with a fistful of flies
and the thought of how the happy families
scattered into the city,

singing, or something like it.

TUESDAY AT THE OFFICE

A human fly has climbed the pylon.
Stripped, but for shoes,
('I hope he gets sunburn,' Sandra says)
he's a cut-out against postcard blue.
We can't hear him, only see mimed anger
as he shouts down to firemen
perched on puny ladders, offering food.
('Waste of public money,' Sandra says)

It's like golf on TV.
We chat, type, photo-copy,
looking up between jobs
at our man, monkeying about.
If he's going to jump, we want to see,
be made solemn, half hoping
it'll make sense of something.
('I know it's a cry for help, but,' Sandra says)

At some point, he's gone.
That night, we watch Thames News
to prove it happened, and we were there.
But there's no mention,
only traffic and a murder,
so he must have climbed quietly
back into his ordinary life.
('I knew he'd let us down,' says Sandra)

WRONG-FOOTED

You're going down a long escalator
into the limbo of the Northern Line,
and despite all gratefully perceived distractions
—a fat balloon-seller gliding upwards,
Kew Gardens poster by a friend of yours—
you can see what's waiting at the bottom is
the subject of an undergraduate essay
you'd get a C for: weigh the respective claims
on the solitary coin that's in your pocket
of the flautist travestying *Summer Time*
and that grey bundle merging with the wall.
Giving to a busker is like shopping
(you're comfortable with that) paying for
a musical snack, instant insouciance;
it's something for something. She looks like your niece.
You don't want the despair of speechless begging
to chill your morning; that belongs outside
the world you think you live in, where one makes
an effort. So that when his body's angles
say life's shit-dark, and some twinge in your bones
says yes, you tell yourself that what you give
someone like that can never be enough,
or the right thing, that only love would do,
and what you've got is one coin in your pocket.
The unsolicited, junk notes sing
put it here . . . *the livin' is easy*. But you're thinking
maybe you shouldn't get by with a neat transaction;
this woman has her flute, and maybe smiles
into the mirror, liking the shape of her chin.
You want to turn and climb towards the light
but you know you'd only stay in the same place
—the thought from which the escalator trips you,
the essay in your head still at page one.

BLURRED VISION

Out in the fast lane, life mimics
going places; no witnesses

to hands slithering on the wheel.
Tear vapour fogs the windscreen as,

on motorways to anywhere, men
cry in their private grief containers.

People they pass might be scandalized
by wide-open mouths boozily singing

but it's desperation unrefined
cracks such large holes in rigid faces.

Maybe they'd want to find themselves
in the hazy place before they were big boys;

but what they see is all one way,
mile upon mile of hard shoulder,

as they're driving, driving much too fast
to notice exits. Alone and dangerous.

OURSTORY

Let us now praise women
with feet glass slippers wouldn't fit;

not the patient, nor even the embittered
ones who kept their place,

but awkward women, tenacious with truth,
whose elbows disposed of the impossible;

who split seams, who wouldn't wait,
take no, take sedatives;

who sang their own numbers, went uninsured,
knew best what they were missing.

Our misfit foremothers are joining forces
underground, their dusts mingling

breast-bone with scapula, forehead
with forehead. Their steady mass

bursts locks; lends a springing foot
to our vaulting into enormous rooms.

THE SMELL OF SWEAT

Sweat is our signature on air:
grapefruit, onions, Glenmorangie.

It is the first date,
the first exam, all firsts;

climb on the cliff path, straining
to work off a terminal prognosis;

rugby hugger-mugger, job well done,
the body throwing out exuberant salts;

nightmare-time—debt, the law,
ex-husband at the door;

one of lust's slippery bouquet
of juices; must of the prison cell.

Its traces swirl around us;
we draw daily breath

from this promiscuous reserve
of extreme moments, not knowing whose.